GW00725938

EASY WALKS

CÔTE D'AZUR
Alpes Maritimes

COMPILED BY
LUC QUISENAERTS

Pre-press & Printing
Grafische Groep Tuerlinckx - Diest/Belgium
ISBN 90-76124-61-2
D/2005/8101/9

© No part of this publication may be reproduce and/or made
public by printing, photocopying, microfilm or in any other
way, without the prior, written consent of D-Publications.

FIRST EDITION

This series fill a gap in the tourist offer of a region. All the walks described in this book are short, easily doable, easily reachable from your holiday accommodation, and they enable you to discover the must beautiful, often hidden spots.

Every one a little gem of discoveries that will give your holiday an extra dimension.

They will provide wonderful impressions, foretastes of all facets, of all the beauty of the landscape, history and culture, that a culture has to offer.

The carefully selected -- and meticulously tended to – walks are offered to you on two to eight pages, with a description of the high points and routes, practical information, maps and many photos.

These guides are designed according to a "zoom-in" structure:

A GENERAL MAP AND THE TABLE OF CONTENTS
- the walks are subdivided and grouped into various tourist regions
  - between Menton and Nice
  - Cannes and the surrounding area

A SECOND MAP FOR EACH REGION
- shows the right location of each walk

PRACTICAL INFORMATION ON THE STROLLS
- highlights
- practical information
- route description
- Many extra photos

I walked through the centuries, along prehistoric sites, Roman diggings, Medieval castles, little Provençal villages, along impressive villas belonging to the rich and famous, both from this century and the preceding one.

I visited unspoilt islets with pure beaches. I also visited an islet that houses one of the most important monasteries of Christian civilization.

I journeyed from subtropical gardens on the banks of the azure-blue sea and from idyllic harbours, right up into the beauty of the alpine mountainscapes, and I was privileged to enjoy the omnipresence of the all-encompassing delights of the picturesque panoramic views of the Mediterranean Sea.

All these discoveries at a stone's throw away from Nice, my abode in this wondrous region ...

CONTENTS

CANNES AND THE SURROUNDING AREA

The "Conservatoire du Littoral"

It is surprising that so much still lays hidden on the French Rivier and the coasts of Provence, so much virginal scenic beauty, spite of the high population density and tourist activity.
This is largely thanks to the "Conservatoire du Littoral".
This is a national French governmental organisation, create by the Act of 10 July 1975, to protect nature throughout Frenc territory (including overseas regions) in the coastal canton along river banks, deltas and the shores of the larger lakes.
In concrete terms, this is done by protecting nature fro unrestrained urbanisation, by maintaining the biodiversit allowing agricultural and fishing activity (albeit controllec and... by opening the sites to the public with footpaths ar signposting (including, sometimes, signs with explanations o the flora, fauna and sites worth seeing.
Many of the strolls described in this guide run through the fascinating sites.
For more information on this organisation, go to ww conservatoire-du-littoral.fr

The "Sentier des Douaniers"

Many miles of promenades along the coasts, which are describ in this guide, are available thanks to the fact that after the Fren revolution, walkways were laid out over the entire length of t French coasts to enable customs patrols to guard the coast a the fight smuggling.

The "Grandes Randonnées" – the « Petites Randonnées »

Hike routes, known as "Grandes Randonnées" or "GR" for sho marked in white and red, run throughout France. In additi to such treks which take several days, there are also what o known as "Petites Randonnées" or "PR" (marked in yello which take only a few hours.

Our "strolls" follow the after indicated routes fully or partia and that is precisely the quality and concept of our routes.

Other information

The strolls vary from visits to gardens, vineyards, and towns, to strolls that take about three hours at most.

Strolls in nature are in theory feasible for and doable by all. Nevertheless, we should point out that a steep stretch emerges here and there, that crags and paths can at times be slippery, and that it is best to take a supply of drinks along. Furthermore, walking shoes are an absolute must.

However, certain nature reserves are not accessible to the public at certain periods (sometimes even from 1 July 2 the 2nd weekend of September), or on certain days (owing to mistral, etc.). Such occasions are clearly posted at the entrance of the strolling estates. To be absolutely certain, you can always get information from the nearest municipal or tourist services.

The route descriptions are subject to change owing to unforeseeable circumstances.

Maps: we advise you to use one of the many Michelin-maps (among others) of the specific areas. Of course a navigationkit will be helpful too, or you can surf to www.michelin.fr.

In this guide we mention for each walk the specific blue topographical IGN-map (www.ign.fr) that you might find in the better travelbook store.

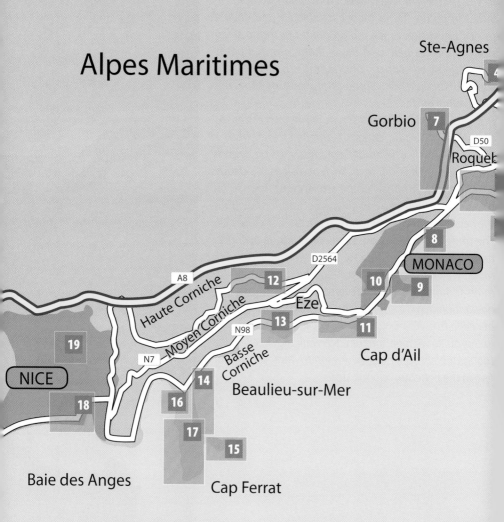

BETWEEN MENTON AND NICE

N

Alpes Maritimes

Ste-Agnes

4

Gorbio

7

D50

Roqueb

8

D2564

MONACO

Haute Corniche

12

10

9

A8

Eze

Moyen Corniche

13

11

N98

Cap d'Ail

19

Basse Corniche

N7

NICE

14

18

Beaulieu-sur-Mer

16

17

15

Baie des Anges

Cap Ferrat

5km

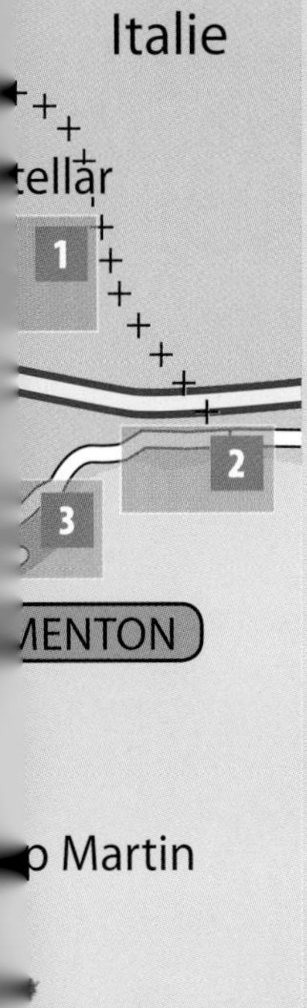

Italie

tellar

1

2

3

ΛΕΝΤΟΝ

ɔ Martin

Between Menton and Nice, the Alps literally hurl themselves in the sea. It is an abrupt transition in nature. Villages that are only a few kilometres from the Mediterranean Sea as the crow flies, often give an Alpine impression. The contrast is so much the more impressive because of the shelter that the high mountain ranges offer the coasts that are orientated directly to the south of them. This results not only in a Mediterranean, but also in a real wondrous subtropical explosion of the beauty of nature.

There is no other place in the world where, a concentration of wealth such as this has seen such unprecedented growth through the passage of time. Think of Monaco, St-Jean-Cap-Ferrat, Cap d'Antibes, Cap Martin, Beaulieu ... But the heritage of the cultural wealth that the region has built up, is insurmountable.

The story of the inn-keeper, that you find in the walk in Saint-Paul-de-Vence, and described in this book, speaks for itself ...

CASTELLAR 1

The panorama Saint-Paul

Castellar is the last village of the Nice hinterland on French soil.

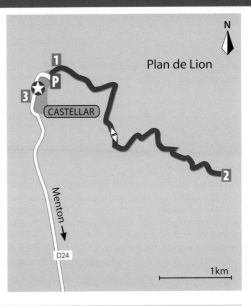

Plan de Lion

CASTELLAR

Menton →

D24

1km

N

tion | Castellar lies 5km north of Menton
IGN 3742 OT
net | search word "Castellar"

the D24 from Menton to Castellar
Park on the parking lot before you
get to the village.

the "Route des granges de Saint-Paul" before the
e, at the chapel of Saint-Sébastien **1**. This runs
wards along the mountain slope of the Plan de Lion, in
rection of the coast, which is about 350 metres below
ou walk until you get to the Saint-Paul **2** farm, where
ad ends. You have a superb panoramic view of Menton
you and of the peninsula Cap-Ferrat in the distance.
along the same road for a visit to the pleasant little
e of Castellar, with its yellow-orange houses.

stellar is the last village of the Nice hinterland on French soil.
narrow little streets and the yellow and ochre-coloured buildings of this eagle's nest above the Gulf of Menton
e a real Italian atmosphere.
ure is also Italian. The Italian-Ligurian Rivièra is, after all, characterized by the steep mountains, foothills of the
s that look as though they are "crashing" into the sea. These steep hills, which are directed due south, are fertile, but
gradient (which can sometimes be as much as 60%!), makes it impossible to cultivate anything naturally. That is
y man has – through the ages and with a great amount of manpower – constructed terraces on which wine, olives,
and citrus fruit are cultivated. Donkeys were used to take stones up to make little walls under one another and in
ween, the soil was levelled out to minute little fields. These "field" terraces sometimes cascade from the mountain
down to the water for hundreds of metres …

2h. 30

The coastal road to Italy

HIGHLIGHTS

- the coastal road with its panoramic view of the Italian and French Rivièra
- panoramic view of the French and Italian Riviera
- prehistoric caves van Balzi Rossi
- the Val Rameh and Pian Park

FACTS

Situation	30km east of Nice. Motorway A8, exit 59 'Menton'
Maps	IGN3742 OT
Internet	www.menton.fr
Telephone	Tourist Office (0033) (0) 492 41 76 76
Route	On the western side of the yacht and fishing harbour of Menton-Garavan (east of the old you have to turn into the Avenue St-Jacques (at a beautiful chapel). You go under the rai line and a few kilometres further up, park at the entrance of the Parc Val Rameh.

ROUTE

After the visit to the botanical garden of Val Rameh **1**, you walk further along the Avenue St-Jacques until you get Bd. de Garavan, where you turn right (50m). The entrance to the olive tree park of "Le Pian" **2** is a little further up. H really feels as though you are in Greece, can you believe! On the south side of the park, there is a walkway, which you over the railway line and so you reach the harbour of Garavan **3**. Then follow the sea bank to the left (eastw You pass the border with italy and in front of the railway bridge, take the Allée Balzi Rossi **4** to the right. Then cro parking lot and go up the footpath along the coast. Walk along the little beach past the prehistoric site of Balzi (which you can visit) and after that, take the coastal path on the right (with the sign Strada interroto a 200m per You walk around the small peninsula and reach the beach with wooden fishers' houses **5**. Return along the same

Jardin du Val Rameh
Exotic, botanical garden of almost 100 years old (1ha) in one of the warmest places on the Rivièra. Because the construction is terraced, one has brilliant views of the sea and Menton. A beautiful avenue, edged by palm trees, leads to the Villa Rameh.

The Caves of Balzi Rossi
Two hundred thousand years ago the homo erectus lived in these (red-coloured) caves. The museum, with its exhibition of archeological finds, gives a good impression of the kind of world these first people inhabited.

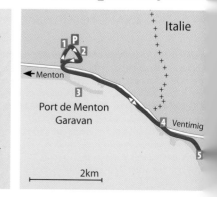

MENTON

The old city

- the Italian holiday atmosphere of Menton
- the unique cemetery

FACTS

Situation	30km east of Nice. Motorway A8, exit 59 'Menton'
maps	IGN3742 OT
	Internet www.menton.fr
Telephone	Tourist Office (0033) (0) 492 41 76 76
Route	Park on the parking lot of the "Plages des Sablettes", which lie next to the old harbour (in direction of Italy)

THE WALK

Walk up the quay in the direction of the sea, and then go up the stairs of Chanoine-Gouget **1** , which take the old city. You now reach the Parvis Saint-Michel **2** , an Italian square that overlooks the harbour and the l' Rivièra. The square is surrounded by pastel-coloured houses and there are two churches with baroque façade first church, the one on the left of the square, is the S-Michel-Archange **3** Basilica. It has a yellow-green façade a opulent interior. Behind it, we find the Chapelle de la Conception **4**, which dates back to 1689 and belonged t Brotherhood of the Black Penitents. Behind this chapel, walk up the Montée du Souvenir **5** on the right, which us to the entrance of the old cemetery **6**.

The graves on this graveyard, which was built on the ruins of a medieval castle in the 19th century, was laid terraces and the graves are grouped according to the nationality of those buried there. The graves are resplen and grandiose, and the site exudes a special atmosphere as a result of the azure sea in the background. Many fa people have been buried here, such s the Delanos, President Roosevelt's family and a few Russian princes. V Montée du Souvenir, we return to the Parvis St-Michel, descend a few steps from the Chanoine-Gouget, an the Rue St-Michel **7** on the right, a pedestrian street with orange trees. We pass the Place des Herbes **8** (on th a Provençal square, complete with arcades and a fountain. Further on, the street has even more belle-époque and it becomes the Avenue Felix Faure, that leads you to the exotic Jardin Biovès **9** and the casino **10** leidt. We along the Promenade du Soleil **11** behind the casino, back to the harbour (notice the lovely covered market behind the Musée Jean Cocteau **12**, we climb the stairs of the Quai Napoléon **13**, the harbour jetty of Menton, which we walk right to the end. This offers us a unique panoramic view of the harbour and the Italian Rivièra. Return until right in front of the Cocteau Museum and walk along the Place des Fours **14** and the Place Bort back to the parking lot.

roughout history, Menton has been hurled backwards and forwards between the Monegasque Grimaldi family, *nce* and the Italian principalities. This was until the population finally pronounced its desire to be attached to *nce*. There are few place on the Rivièra where the climate is so soft and the vegetation so lusciously sub-tropical. *reover, every year the famous lemon festivities are held here in February, a festivity where 100 ton of citrus fruit is *ed* to portray certain themes.

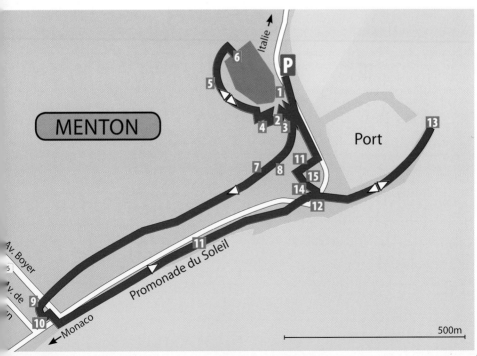

Village on the French coast

HIGHLIGHTS

- the medieval garden in the castle's ruins
- the mighty fort
- the unspoilt panoramic views

FACTS

Situation	10km north of Menton
Maps	IGN 3742 OT
Internet	www.sainteagnes.fr
Route	from the N7, take the D22 between Menton and Roquebrune, in the direction of Sainte-Ag Park on the parking lot on the northern side of the villiage on the Place des Combattants.

THE WALK

You walk along the Place de l'Eglise **1**. Walk straight ahead through the little high street to the Place du Châte where you take the path upwards to the ruins of the castle and the medieval garden (Jardin Médieval) **3**. The med garden was a project undertaken by the Association des Peintres du Soleil and one can visit the garden after h given a donation towards the renovation of the ruins (you can give as much or little as you please). After the take the same way back to the Place du Château. Left, southwards, you see the fort of the Ligne Maginot **4** (visi allowed). Under the fort there is a terrace that provides a wonderful view of the coast.
Return the same way.

Sainte-Agnes is a real eagle's nest: it lies at three kilometres from the coast, as the crow flies, and at a height of 800 metres! Needless to say, one can enjoy the most extraordinary panoramic views. The height and the view were also important from a militarily strategic point of view and from the 12th century, the medieval castle, which is built an even higher 180 metres above the village, kept watch over the whole coast around Menton, the border area between the French Kingdom and the Italian principalities. Immediately under the castle, on the south side of the village, is the last fort of the Maginot lline, built between 1932 and 1938. It is an unbelievably impressive building as a whole, which has been completely carved out of the rocks. 300 soldiers could function completely autonomously, in that mighty structure, which had an own electricity power station, dormitories, kitchens and even a sick berth with operating theatre.

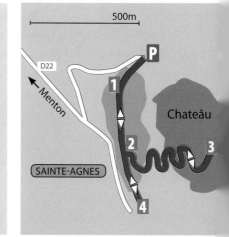

HIGHLIGHTS

- the age-old olive trees in the park
- the peninsula's residential character

FACTS

Situation	between Monaco and Menton
Maps	IGN 3742 OT
Internet	www.roquebrune-cap-martin.com, "search word "Cap Martin"
Telephone	Tourist office (0033) (0) 493 35 62 87
Route	Take the N7 to Cap Martin from Monaco or Menton, and after that the Avenue Paul-Doume to the Parc du Cap Martin (at the town hall, "la Mairie"). Park here.

THE WALK

Walk through the beautiful Cap Martin **1** park, with its age-old olive trees and go to via the Avenue Virginie-Heri a westerly direction until you get to the hotel Europe-Village **3**. Pass the entrance of the hotel and take the step descend to the sea. (Sentier de la Dragonnière). Follow the lovely path left along the coast, that runs along gr domains and villas all round the Cap Martin peninsula. You pass the Casa del Mar **4** beach paviljoen and very you will have a view of the Italian Rivièra. Here you will also pass the bust of one of its most famous inhabitant architect, Le Corbusier **5**. When you reach the tarred road again (in front of the restaurant Cap Martin), take it left. Turn left (Avenue W. Churchill), pass the Grand Hôtel **6** and go back to the parc du Cap Martin via the A Doumer.

This walk starts in the park of Cap Martin, famous for its age-old, scary olive trees, and then goes on along the Sentier des Douaniers (the customs path) all round the Cap, and passes the gardens and villas of distinguished people, because when the jet-set of yesteryear found out that Empress Sissi regularly walked along this path, everyone wanted a villa here ...

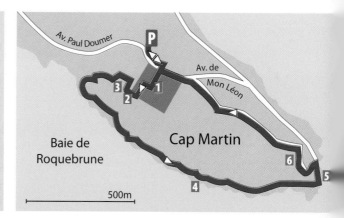

Charles-Edouard JEANNERET
dit "Le Corbusier"
1887 - 1965
Architecte
Enterré au cimetière
de Roquebrune Cap-Martin

HIGHLIGHTS

- Le Corbusier's little hut
- the beautiful, historical village of Roquebrune
- the panoramic views

FACTS

Situation	between Monaco and Menton
Maps	IGN 3742 OT
Internet	www.roquebrune-cap-martin.com, "search word "Cap Martin"; "Roquebrune", "Le Corbusier
Telephone	Tourist Office (0033) (0) 493 35 62 87
Route	Take the N7 from Monaco or Menton to Cap Martin, and then the Avenue Paul-Doumer u the Parc du Cap Martin (at the town hall, "la Mairie"). Park here.

THE WALK

Walk through the beautiful Cap Martin park **1** with its age-old olive trees and go via de Avenue Virginie-Heriot **2** westerly direction until you get to the hotel Europe-Village **3**. Pass the entrance of the hotel and take the steps descend to the sea. (Sentier de la Dragonnière). From here, follow the lovely coastal path to the right, in the dire of Monaco. You go past Le Corbusier's hut **4** (have a good look on your left). A little further on, on the right-hand you will see a tunnel under a railway line. You go under this tunnel and follow the path upwards. You cross the N7 follow the Montée Corinthille **5** to Roquebrune on the other side. You cross the D50 and follow the path further the "village" upwards. You get to the medieval village centre of Roquebrune, more specifically, the Rue de l'Eglis the left you can go to the Place des Deux Frères, with its age-old olive trees and the beautiful panoramic view, ly

the foot of the castle. Via the Rue Grimaldi, you go to the Rue Moncollet. This picturesque little street has narrow, long, covered alleys with steps. The street has been carved into the rock and leads to the Rue du Château and the castle. You go back to the Rue de l'Eglise, and in front of the church you go left into the the little street with steps and you take the Rue de la Fontaine on the right. You get to a square and follow straight ahead, in the direction of "Olivier Millenaire". You pass the 1000-year-old olive tree **6**. Further on, just behind the chapel Saint-Roch **7**, go to the right towards the coast, by following the sign "Cap Martin". At the N7, take left (20m) and then to the right (Av. Gén. Leclerc).This road you follow till the end (D52), and here to the left (sign "Mairie – Avenue Doumer).

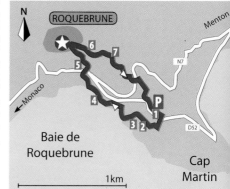

To the Mont Gros.

HLIGHTS

the little mountain village of Gorbio
the panoramic views from the Mont Gros

'S

ation	Gorbio lies about 8km north of Roquebrune-Cap Martin
s	IGN 3742 OT
net	search word "Gorbio"
e	follow the D50 from Roquebrune to Gorbio. Park as near as possible to the centre.

WALK

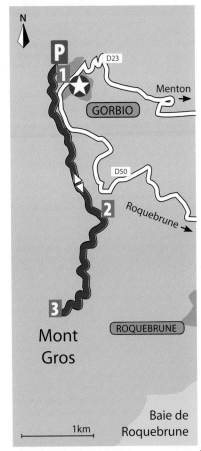

nter the little village via a lovely square, the Place des Victoires **1**. walk through a gate and enter the medieval centre. You can freely this small, hitherto unspoilt village with its narrow streets and tiful houses that date back to between the 11th and the 17th uries. The walk starts on the other side of the Place des Victoires, d the corner. You follow the arrows "Mont Gros GR51" the ue Verdun. You climb along the mountain slope and you have ely view of the village. On top of the, **2** the sea dooms up before and you follow the signs that are marked "Cime de Mont Gros". On ime de Mont Gros, **3** you are rewarded with a sublime panoramic of the coast. Return the same way you came.

rbio lies right near the Mediterranean Sea, but already the village an alpine character and atmosphere.It lies in a enormous and ndiose frame of high mountains. On the Day of the Sacraments, "snail procession" is held here. The inhabitants who take part in procession then carry oil lamps made out of snails' shells. All the dow sills and thresholds are also lit up with thousands of lights nails' shells.

39

The Japanese garden and the Promenade des Champions

HIGHLIGHTS

- the atmosphere in the Japanese garden
- Larvotto, the only beach of the principality of Monaco

FACTS

Situation	east of the harbour of Monaco
Maps	IGN 3742 OT
Internet	www.monaco-tourisme.com
Telephone	Tourist Office (00377) (0) 92 16 61 16
Route	follow the direction "Menton" from the centre of Monaco until you get to the Larvotto sub Park on one of the parking lots. The Japanese garden lies next to the parade (next to Atrium).

THE WALK

Walk of your own choice through the 0.7ha-sized Japanese garden **1**. The Promenade des Champions **2** and wa the Méridien Beach Palace **3** hotel. Return the way you came.

The Japanese garden

This exceptional garden lies at the seaside, in the suburb of Larvotto, east of the harbour, in the direction of Menton and Cap Martin, next to the Larvotto beach, the only beach in Monaco. The garden portrays a mini Shinto image of "nature", with, among others, the three principles that go to form the Japanese garden, namely, the "line" (a broad avenue), the "area" (the waterfall) and the "point" (the pond). Much symbolism has been integrated in the garden, which, is unknown to westerners: So, for example, the walkway symbolizes the difficult passage to the realm of the gods, the little island with the two exotic pine trees, is in the shape of a tortoise and symbolizes "longevity", the ellipses in the gravel refer to the eternal movement of the universe, whereas the Japanese tea house provides the place as a whole with a more worldly tint.

the "Larvotto" suburb

Even according to Monagesque standards, this is exclusive. Here one does not have – because of the open sea, the beach and the parade – the impression of being completely locked in. There is a cosy, nonchalant, holiday atmosphere.

MONACO

"Le Rocher" - the old city

INFO

- the oceanografic museum
- a real miniature operette state

FACTS

Situation	in the centre of Monaco, between the harbour and the suburb of Fontvieille
Maps	IGN 3742 OT
Internet	www.monaco-tourisme.com, search word "Monaco"
Telephone	Tourist Office (00377) (0) 92 16 61 16
Route	In Monaco, follow the signs to "Le Rocher". The road ends at the parking lots.

THE WALK

You reach the parking lot and you follow the banks to the right. The monumental Musée Océanographique **1** rise in front of you. You take the lifts or the escalator to the old city and you come to the square in front of this mus This museum, which belongs to one of the most important oceanografic museums in the world, was establishe Prince Albert I, who was enormously interested in the science of the sea, in 1910. It houses, amongst others, a interesting a aquarium. (After a possible visit), you walk along the Jardins St-Martin **2** to the cathedral **3** that was in neo-Roman style at the end of the 19th century. Via the Rue du Colonel de Castro you reach the square in of the palace **4**. One can visit a great part of the Prince's palace, such as the Hercule hall with frescoes from the century and the throne hall where the wedding between Rainier and Grace Kelly took place.
The Musée des Souvenirs Napoléoniens is also housed in this palace. Via the Rue Basse you come to the 17th ce. chapel of the Miséricorde **5**. You walk to the city hall that stands straight opposite the chapel. At the city ha follow the Rue Emile de Loth to the left until you get to the Place de la Visitation **6**. Here you walk right, downwar the square and up again for the oceanografic museum.

The principality of Monaco is divided into four parts: from east to west : Monte Carlo, the neighbourhood around het Casino; La Condamine, around and behind the harbour, the "Rock", that houses the old city and the palace, a Fontvieille, the new residential neighbourhood with its yacht harbour.
This walk leads us through the "Rock" - "Le Rocher". This 300-metre-broad mountain protrudes 800 metres high fr the sea and, see from a militarily strategic point of view, it was very useful. The atmosphere in the salmon-colou old city is really unique (at least, if there are not too many tourists) : you feel and you see that you are walking i miniature operette state. The little streets, squares and buildings look as if they have been snatched away fro theatre decor. Everything is 18th and 19th century, but extremely well cared for and newly painted. The impressio reinforced by the square in front of the palace where two soldiers stand guard in front of the gate. The Place du Pa is littered with canon and piled canon balls, a gift to the Grimaldis from Lous XIV, King of France.

he Grimaldi dynasty

1297 François Grimaldi, a Genoese, together with a few soldiers, conquered Monaco by disguising themselves as
onks. To this day, the Grimaldis have two armed monks on their coat of arms. However, in 1308 Monaco was bought
 another Grimaldi from Genoa, and it is this generation that is still on the throne.

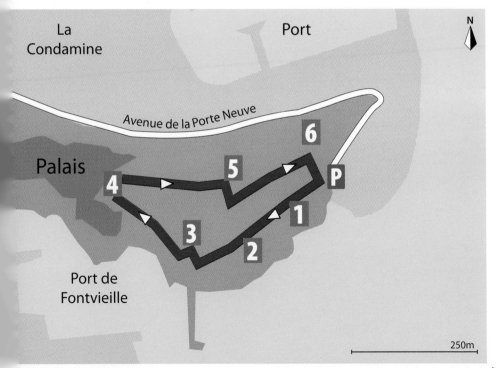

The Exotic Garden

HLIGHTS

the exotic plant species
the panoramic view of the "Rock"

TS

ation	above the "Rocher" of Monaco
s	IGN 3742 OT
net	www.monaco-tourisme.com, www.jardin-exotique.mc, search word "Monaco", "Jardin exotique Monaco"
hone	Tourist Office 00377) (0) 92 16 61 16
e	situated on the Moyenne Corniche, on the Boulevard du Jardin Exotique (follow the signs). Park at 100 metres from the entrance. From the down-town area (more specifically from the entrance of the Princess Grace Hospital on the Avenu Pasteur) one can also go to the garden with a lift (it is marked).

WALK

of your own choice, during which you descend to the
rvatoire cave along winding paths in the garden, and
er on to the archeological museum.

The Exotic Garden
These are gardens hanging on a steep rock face above the sea, facing due south. All exotic species, from Mexican, over South African to Asian species, thrive in this micro-climate. You walk between a collection totalling 7000 tropical plants, that are sometimes giant-sized and take on bizarre shapes .
From the gardens you have a view of the old city of Monaco and the harbour of Fontvieille, a view that goes beyond your vision.

The "de l'Observatoire" cave
Below the gardens there are sixty metres of deep caves with stalagtites and stalagmites. It is the only cave in Europe where it gets warmer as one descends deeper into it. People lived her about 200,000 years ago. The objects that were found here are exhibited in the museum.

The anthropoligical museum
This lies behind the cave. In this interesting museum, we discover evidence of the different climate changes in these regions in the course of time. So, for example, skeletons of mammoths and reindeer that lived here during the Ice Ages, as well as skeletons of elephants and rhinoceroses from the warm periods of time, have been dug up here. Furthermore, the museum gives an overview of the development of humanity, with, amongst others, skeletons of the homo sapiens.

HIGHLIGHTS

- the paradise beach of Mala
- the coastal road with its panoramic views
- the Sasha Guitry park

FACTS

Situation	Cap Mala lies between Beaulieu and Monaco
Maps	IGN 3742 OT
Internet	search word "Cap d'Ail"
Route	You come from Beaulieu-sur-Mer, via the N98, and you park as closely as possible to roundabout before the centre of Cap d'Ail.

The exclusive atmosphere and the discretion of the resort has always attracted the greates of the world, such as t[...] Tsar of Russia, Greta Garbo and Cocteau. Thanks to the coastal road, we can all now enjoy the beauty and the pe[...] and quiet of this earthly paradise.

THE WALK

At the roundabout, you walk along the Avenue Charles Banc in the direction of the sea (signs with "Eden Résid[...] and "Plage Mala"). At the Résidence Eden **1**, you go to the right of the domain and follow the way that makes [...] turn downwards. Via a path of steps, you reach the hidden, paradise beach of Mala **2** with its restaurant and beach infrastructure. On the left, at the end of the beach, you follow the coastal road that runs along Cap Mala to the open sea. You walk up the rock path along the residential domains with beautiful gardens. The path is very well looked after with pic-nic infrastructure and signs with explanation. You pass Cap Rognoso **3** and reach Cap d'Ail **4**. Return the same way until you get to the thoroughfare on the left to the Avenue Gramaglia and the Sasha Guitry Park **5**. It is wonderful to saunter in this Mediterranean park of the famous actor and author. Then you carry on and follow the Avenue Gramaglia, which winds upwards between the gardens to the Eden Résidence. Return along the same route.

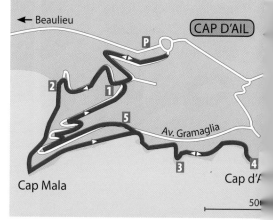

HIGHLIGHTS

- the demarcated nature walks
- the sublime panoramic views of the coast

FACTS

Situation	a few kilometres west of La Turbie, above the Haute Corniche.
Maps	IGN 3742 OT
Internet	www.eze-riviera.com
Route	Take the D2564 from La Turbie D2564 in the direction of Eze (Haute Corniche). After a kilometres, you see arrows to the "Parc de la Revère » on the right. The road winds upwa Park at the fort, right at the top.

THE WALK(S)

-A La Simboula (1 hour)
From the fort your follow the botanical route to the orientation table of Simboula. The route has been marked
arrows. Return along the signposted path that leads northwards along panoramic views (ornithological observ.
tower).

-B Cime de la Forna (2 ½ hours)
The walk to the Cime de la Forna on the plateau of the Parc Départemental de la Grande Corniche also leaves
the fort.

Both walks are well signposted.

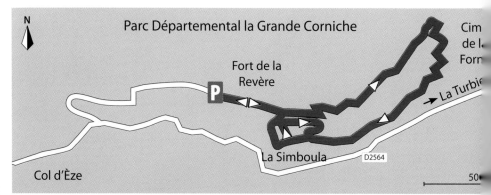

The Sentier Nietsche

HIGHLIGHTS

- gradually climb up to one of the most beautiful places above the Côte d'Azur

This footpath inspired the German philosopher, Friedrich Nietzsche, to write his masterpiece "Also sprach Zarathoestra".
The path descends from the village of Eze, among olive and pine trees, down to the coast, more specifically to the beach that has also been named after him.
The eagle's nest of Eze, a Celtic-Ligurian settlement, where Phoenicians, Romans and Saracenes lived successively, is situated on the peninsula of Saint-Jean-Cap-Ferrat.
A reinforced gater from the 14th century offers access to the village. The village has been beautifully renovated and the shops and many little galleries ooze refinement. The splendrous flowers around and on the renovated little houses are overwhelming and, while one is sauntering through the little cobbled streets, you regularly get surprising views of the sea and the mountains. Right at the top of the village we find the exotic garden, planted on what was left over of a 14th century castle, which was demolished by order of Louis XIV. The panoramic view of the Riviera from the terrace of the garden is superb. Do not forget to walk along the very beautiful 18th century pastel-coloured church. The façade is classisistic and in the baroque interior there is a remarkable 18th century statue that represents Our Lady's Assumption into Heaven and is attributed to Muerto.

FACTS

Situation	Eze-Bord-de-Mer lies on the coast, or N98 between Beaulieu-sur-Mer and Cap
Maps	IGN 3742 OT
Internet	www.eze-riviera.com
Route	from Beaulieu or Cap d'Ail, drive to Bord-de-Mer and park at the station.

THE WALK

From the station, walk up the N98 in the direction of Cap opwandelen richting Cap d'Ail. After 100m, take the "Se Nietsche" 1 left. This gradually climbs between the villas runs below the rock through the thicket to the little vall the Duc, to end up at the foot of the village of Eze 2. Vi your choice in Eze. Return along the same route.

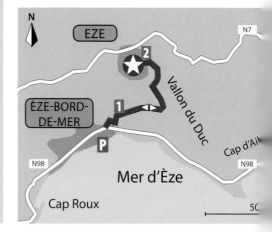

The Promenade Maurice Rouvier

HIGHLIGHTS

• walk on one of the most exclusive little places in the world.

FACTS

Situation	Beaulieu-sur-Mer lies on the east side of the Cap-Ferrat peninsula
Internet	www.ot-beaulieu-sur-mer.fr
Maps	IGN 3742 OT
Route	park at the Beaulieu casino.

THE WALK

You walk from the casino **1** to the right and up the beach parade. The path runs along the coast, between the water and the villas, via the Pointe Rompa Talon **2** right to the yacht harbour of Saint-Jean-Cap-Ferrat **3**. Return along the same route.

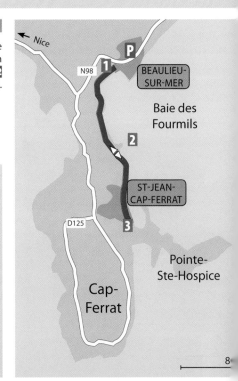

The name says it itself: « lovely place » !
Beaulieu is not only one of the most beautiful places on the Riviera, but it also enjoys a very mild climate and a luscious sub-tropical vegetation, thanks to the shelter the steep hills provide agains the wind and the cold from the north.
It was no-one less than Napoleon who gave the city its name, when he called out: "qual bel luogo!", on his visit to the city, which, at the time, was Corsican for "what a beautiful place!".
This walk takes us to the yacht harbour of Saint-Jean-Cap-Ferrat, along the banks of the Baie des Fourmis, whick evokes a nostalgic atmosphere with its belle-époque houses, its palm trees and beautiful gardens.

Pointe Ste-Hospice

HOOGTEPUNTEN

- This will turn out to be a walk on a peninsula on a peninsula (no, this is not a typing error!)…

FACTS

Situation	the little harbour of Saint-Jean-Cap-Ferrat lies on the east side of the peninsula of Cap-Ferra
Maps	IGN 3742 OT
Internet	search word « Cap-Ferrat »
Route	Follow the signposting Villefranche or Beaulieu. Park in the harbour of St-Jean.

THE WALK

From the harbour of St-Jean 1, follow the road to Ste-Hospice along the Palace de la Voile d'Or. You then come crossroads above the Plage de la Fossettes. Continue straight ahead for 100 metres further, and you will find a staircas your left. This leads to the Paloma Beach 2. Continue following the beach and take the coastal stone road. This path leads to the Pointe Sainte-Hospice 3 and then down westwards to the Pointe du Colombier 4. Here, on your right, yo find a path (that has been marked) that will lead you to the Ste-Hospice Chapel 5. You follow the tarred road, whic many bends, upwards to the chapel. Take the same way back to the sea and, when you get back to the crossroads, fe along the Bay of Les Fossettes on the right-hand side. Via the Avenue Claude-Vignon, you get back to St-Jean-Cap-Fe

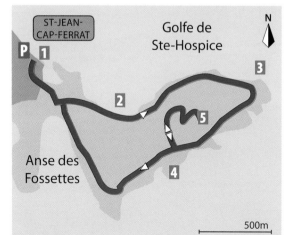

This will turn out to be a walk on a penins on a peninsula (no, this is not a typi error!)…
From the beach of Paloma we follow the coas road between the villas and the sea, which off wonderful panoramic views of the beach of French and Italian Riviera, and of the rest of C Ferrat. Furthermore, we also walk to the chape Sainte-Hospice, on the top of the hill. This cha is dominated by a gigantic eleven-metre-h statue of the Madonna and Child.
The chapel was built in honour of Saint Hospit He was a monk took it upon himself to pray to C on the part of the fishermen and all the peopl the neighbourhood, who had to work to surv and who had hardly any time to pray.

Villa Ephrussi-Rothschild

a unique villa, with a unique garden, and situated in a ... unique place !

TS

ation	on the St-Jean-Cap-Ferrat peninsula.
s	IGN 3742 OT
rnet	www.ephrussi.com
te	drive up the peninsula (Avenue de Grasse) from Villfranceor Beaulieu. The villa is signposted a little further on (on the left). Park in front of the villa.

THE WALK

You first walk through the villa itself. After that, you get to the garden via the south terrace. You first go right, behind the corner, where the tearoom is housed and you follow the route.

In the beginning of the 20th century Baroness Ephrussi de Rothschild had a superb palazzo built in Florentine-Moorish style on top of the narrowest part of the Saint-Jean-Cap-Ferrat peninsula. She called the villa "Ile de France", after the fantastic memories that she had from her cruise with the same name.

She housed her gigantic art collection in the villa: five thousand masterpieces, which can still be admired there. Behind the palazzo, the Baroness had a garden of seven hectares laid out, each in a separate style : a Florentine, a rockery, a Spanish, a Japanese, an exotic French, a Provençal garden, and a rosarium. Both the villa and the gardens look out onto both the Bay of Villefranche in the west and the Bay of Beaulieu in the east.

In 1934 she donated the whole heritage to the Institut de France, which made a museum of it.

Walk around the peninsula

HIGHLIGHTS

- panoramic views all around you in full circle, of one of the moste exclusive places in the world.

FACTS

Situation	the little harbour of Saint-Jean-Cap-Fe lies on the east side of the Cap-Fe peninsula.
Maps	IGN 3742 OT
Internet	search word "Saint-Jean-Cap-Ferrat"
Route	from Villefranche or Beaulieu, drive up peninsula (D25). A little after you have pas the sign, go left to the Villa Ephrussi Rothschild, take the road on the right, wh leads to the beach, to the "Plage de Passab

THE WALK

From this lovely beach **1** with its view of the Bay of Villefranche, left, further up the peninsula. A little further on, you have to p block of flats and behind it you will find the coastal road, which can follow to the most extreme point of Cap Ferrat Cap-Ferrat. there is the lighthouse **2**. The path then turns to the eastern of the Cap, along the bare rocks of the Pointe Causinière **3**, and swimming pool of the Grand Hôtel du Cap Ferrat. Then pass the harbour of Fosses **4**. Via de Avenue Claude Vignon, you get to harbour of St-Jean **5**. You walk along the quay and climb westw along the Avenue Denis Séméria. You get to the D25, which take to the right for a little while. After that, follow the road aga the left, which goes descends down to the Passable.

This scary, but wonderful peninsula lies like a shrine in a protected area, inbedded between the Bays of Villefranche a Beaulieu-sur-Mer. There are few places on earth where so much wealth has gathered during the last few centuries. Leopold II of Belgium competed with the Rothschild family when it came to pomp and circumstance. The fishing harbour of Saint-Jean-Cap-Ferrat, with its many yachts lies discretely hidden in the Bay of Sainte-Hosp and provides unspoilt panoramic views of both the French and Italian Riviera.

Vieux Nice

- a surprising city walk through the centuries

FACTS

Maps	IGN 3742 OT
Internet	www.nicetourism.com
Telephone	(0033) (0) 492 14 48 00
Route	At the coast, on the Promenade des Anglais, park on one of the parking lots around the Jard Albert I.

THE WALK

From the Jardin Albert I **1**, walk eastwards up the sea parade, the Quai des Etats-Unis (the Promenade des Anglais actually only begins on the western side of the Jardin Albert I). At the end of the beach, you see a lift in the rock face on the left **2** (ascenseur), which takes you to the castle hill. When you get to the top, you walk to the right, into the park. On the east side, you can enjoy a lovely view **3** of the old harbour of Nice. You walk back in the direction of the lift, then to the right, and take the path downwards in front of the castle ruins. You pass the waterfall that cascades down on the right of the mountain. Then you get to a graveyard **4** (which you can visit during opening hours), and in front of the graveyard you descend the little street with steps (Montée Menica Rondelli), down to the old city. You get to the convent de la Visitation **5** on the Place du Carret. You take a few narrow streets to the right, the Rue de la Providence, the Rue Zanin and the Rue Pairolaire, and so you reach the Bd Gén. Leclerc, with the Place Garibaldi **6** on the right. After that you go back via the Rue Pairolière, but you continue walking straight ahead. You pass the Place Saint-François **7** (on the right) and at the fork, you take the right fork, the Rue Droite **8**, a little street with many small art galleries. You pass the Place Jésus **9**, a brilliant Italian square with many terraces and restaurants, until you get to the T-junction, where you take the Rue de la Préfecture to the right **10**, until you get to the Place du Palais de Justice **11**. Via the Rue de la Terrasse, you get to the Cours Saleya **12**, a long, stretched-out Italian square where there is a daily flower, vegetable and herb market. Right at the end of this square, back at the rock on which the castle is situated, you turn right under the gate of the parade, which you follow to the right until you reach the Jardin Albert I.

400m

Av. J. Médecin

Baie

…e old part of the city of Nice lies at the foot of the castle hill and is further enclosed by the Quai des Etats-Unis at …e beach and the long stretch of green oasis of the Jardin Albert I and the Place Masséna. In the early Middle ages all …habitants lived on the hill around the castle, but from the 13th century, the city expanded to the west at sea level, and …the centuries that followed, the old city acquired its present-day appearance. Until 1860, Nice was an Italian city, …der the rule of the House of Savoie, which is very noticeable in the inner city. The houses in the narrow, picturesque cities are pastel-shaded, the washing hangs out to dry on the balconies and on the squares with fountains and arcades, there are beautiful baroque churches, chapels and pallazzi.

Vieux Nice bustles with Mediterranean life : the little shops in the little streets are often half on the street, without shop windows. Thousands of people do their daily shopping the the Cours Saleya, market and there are innumerable little terraces and open-air restaurants practically the whole year round.

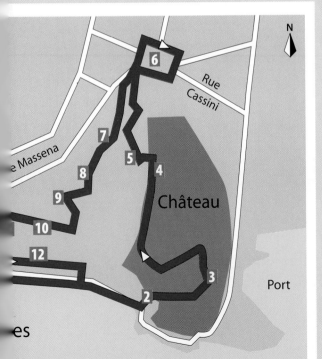

Cimiez

- visit to an unknown, but extremely diverse heritage, that encompasses 2,600 years of history.

FACTS

Situation	a northern suburb of Nice
Maps	IGN 3742 OT
Internet	www.nicetourism.com, search word "Cimiez"
Telephone	(0033) (0) 492 14 48 00
Route	from the centre of Nice, the A8 in the direction of Nice-Nord. Then follow the signs "Cir Parkin the Avenue du Monastère.

THE WALK

This residential neighbourhood of Nice has Roman springs and an arena **1** that provided room for 4,000 specta The many arteFACTS that have been dug up lie exhibited in the archeological museum of Cimiez **2** (the Latin r is Cemenelum).

The Gallo-roman site **3** is situated between the archeological museum and the museum of Matisse. In the century A.D., Cemenelum had about 20,000 inhabitants.

Then our walk takes us to the 16th century, where we visit a beautiful Franciscan monastery **4**. This houses a museum that gives an overview of these monks' life and way of living through the centuries. The wonderfully beautiful terrace-shaped garden of the monastery looks out on the city.

And our visit to Cimiez ends in the 16th cnetury Italian patrician house where the Matisse museum **5** is housed. It is with about thirty paintings that the evolution of the painter's style throughout the years, is depicted: from his initial, "dark" period to his last works that are drenched in Mediterranean light…

Walk of your own choice.

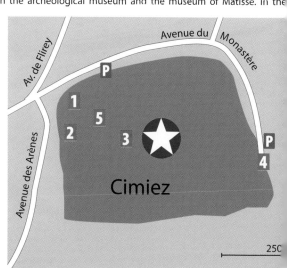

CANNES AND THE SURROUNDING AREA

NICE

es

Cannes? The film festival! Where Nice and the surrounding area used attract the jet-set fifty to a hundred years ago, Cannes is more focused on the here and now. Although ... Saint-Honorat, an island very near the coast of this mundane city, houses one of the most important monasteries from the early Christian civilization, and the region was, for centuries, the border – and disputed territory – between the Italian and the Monacan principalities and the kingdom of France. Napoleon set foot on land again inGolfe-Juan after he had escaped from his place of exile, Elba, and wild horses could not drag Picasso away from Antibes and Mougins, where he painted some of his most beautiful paintings.

Léopold II of Belgium felt like the "King of kings" inCap d'Antibes, so to speak. Renoir peace and inspiration in Cagnes ... Grasse is THE perfume city of the world. Therefore, what history, what wealth!

HIGHLIGHTS

- climbing the most beautiful and largest "Baou" in southern France
- the panoramic views of the coast
- the Provençal village of Saint-Jeannet

FACTS

Situation	about 10km east of Vence, and 15km west of Carros
Maps	IGN 3643 ET
Internet	www.saintjeannet.com
Route	take the D2210 from Carros, in the direction of Vence. Follow the arrows to Saint-Jeannet. on the parking lot on the left-hand side, in front of the village.

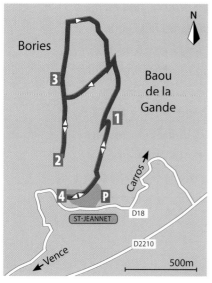

THE WALK

Walk into the village. From the village, you will find different a (on the right) that show the way to the beginning of the w the "Baou van Saint-Jeannet". You follow the rocky path up the valley of Parriau **1** (the GR-51, red and white). On this the municipality put up signs giving an explanation of the p in our solar system. At a certain point, you will have to lea GR path by turning sharp left, in the direction of the Baou. T-junction, you keep to the left and in this way you read orientation table of the Baou **2**. There is brilliant panorami of the coast, from before Cagnes-sur-Mer, the plain in front village of Saint-Jeannet, up to the Estérel Massif and the na park of Mercantour on the Italian border.

Return the same way to the fork, and then continue straight a You cross sink-hole plateau **3** , and pass a few ruins of "t barns and shepherds' houses. You reach the GR path once which you take to the right to go into the village. Do not fo explore the village further after your walk. It is really worth what with the Provençal washing place and, further on, whe have walked through the whole village, the Notre Dam Champs **4** chapel.

The "baous"

"baou" is the Provençal word for imposing, chopped-off mountain. There are four in this area. The Baou of Sa Jeannet is 800 metres high and on the south side, it has an almost vertical rock face of 200 metres high.

The upland-plain of Noves

HIGHLIGHTS

- an impressive sink-hole plateau, which you would not expect, so near to the Mediterranean Sea.

FACTS

Situation	Le Plan des Noves lies about 8km north of Vence
Maps	IGN 3643 ET
Internet	search word "Plan des Noves"
Route	From Vence, follow the D2 in the direction of Col de Vence. Park on the parking lot of Le Plan Noves, a few kilometres from the top.

THE WALK

From the parking lot, follow the arrows to the Plan des Noves (eastwards). You follow the GR path (red and whit the next post with signposting **1** (sign 65). Here, you take the GR path to the left. About 350 metres further dow sign 65A, follow to the right: "circuit Plan des Noves" **2**. At the fork in the road, keep to the left and climb the rid an easterly direction. You pass the ruins of barns **3** and the road bends southwards. You continue walking on the r which now turns to the right. On your right, you see the ruins of a shepherd's dwelling. This place is called Mangia **4**. A bit further on, you get to yet another signpost **5**. Here, you continue following the "circuit Plan des Noves" t next post, which you passed previously when you came. Return the same way.

From Vence, the path winds to the Col de Vence. The natural vegetation changes with every bend. The Mediterranean character is completely lost and you could make the mistake of thinking that you are on a Scottish Highland. The sink-hole plateaus above Vence were used as barns where grain was stored in bygone days, but they are now completely deserted and classified as a nature park.

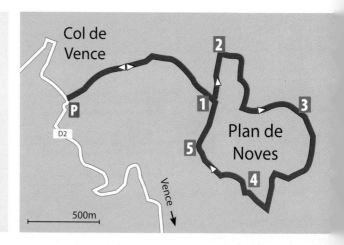

HIGHLIGHTS

- Saint-Paul-de-Vence : THE arists' village par excellence !

FACTS

Maps	IGN 3643 ET
Internet	www.saint-pauldevence.com, www.fondation-maeght.com
Route	from the A8 Nice-Cannes, take the exit Cagnes-sur-Mer, and then follow the signposting Ve and Saint-Paul-de-Vence. Park on one of the parking lots at the entrance to the village.

THE WALK

You walk into the village through the gate and follow the Rue Grande 2, a pedestrian street with art galleries both left and r
You walk right to the end of this picturesque street (but do not forget the side streets, because they are also beautiful!). Ther
reach the Place du Trincol 3, where you climb up the village walls. You have a beautiful view of the idyllic surrounding area.
you walk on the village walls 4 and back to the entrance to the village, with a view of the gardens of Saint-Paul on your left.
on the road (the D7), you will see a chapel in front of you 5, on the opposite side of the street. Take the path going up, left c
chapel. Behind you, you have a unique panoramic view of Saint-Paul-de-Vence. You follow this path, which descends again,
you reach the place where it crosses the road. On the opposite side (walk a little to the right) is the entrance to the Fond;
Maeght 6 on the hill of Les Gardettes. You walk through the park to the museum (which you can visit). Return the same wa

The Fondation Maeght
Aimé Maeght was a fervent of Miro, as well as a passionate art lover. In the beginning of the 60s, he had a museum built, of whi
the building is a great piece of art in itself! Many artists collaborated on this masterpiece : Pol Bury with his fountains, Braque
the glass frame, Miro with ceramics … The museum houses the world's most valuable collections from the 20th century : Tapi
Matisse, Léger … you find works of art by all the greatest artists.

The La Colombe d'Or Inn
A little over a hundred years ago, all kinds of painters from the coast moved to the interior to take advantage of the colours and light and to glean inspiration for their work. Sometimes they had enough money to stay in the Inn, sometimes not. That is why the innkeeper gave them accommodation in return for a painting. In this way, Miro, Picasso and Signac in La Colombe d'Or stayed at the inn and made their masterpieces. Even to this day, the inn, which has expanded into a luxury hotel, is still in the hands of the same family, namely the Roux family, and the paintings are still there. Some of them are paintings of great value.

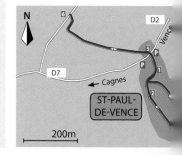

HIGHLIGHTS

- an unrivalled view of Haut-de-Cagnes
- the romantic atmosphere in the park and in the museum

FACTS

Maps	IGN 3643 ET
Internet	www.cagnes-tourisme.com, search word "Auguste Renoir"
Route	Follow the signs to the "Musée Renoir" from the centre of Cagnes. When you drive from N to Cannes, or vice versa, via the N7, and near the little harbour of Cros de Cagnes, you sho follow the direction of Les Collettes and "Musée Renoir" (Avenue Besset). Parkin front of entrance.

THE WALK

Walk of your own choice through the park and the museum.

In 1903, Renoir (1841-1919), one of the founders of impressionism, bought a domain with an unobstructed view of Haut-de-Cagnes. The park measured two hectares and is planted with in 16th century olive groves. It is an idyllic, romantic garden, where Renoir put his easel in every little corner and where he drew portraits of his postmen. It was on this estate that he also painted his greatest work, one of which was Les Grandes Baigneuses (the "Bathers"), and it was here that he entertained famous artists such as Modigliani, Matisse and Rodin. He stayed there until his death in 1919.

In the garden in front of the mansion, between the orange trees, stands the famous statue of Venus Vitrix, that he made together with his friend, Guino.

The house itself, where the museum is housed, has remained unchanged. All his furniture is still in the same place, as are his easels in his painting studios. About ten of the painter's own works are still there to be admired.

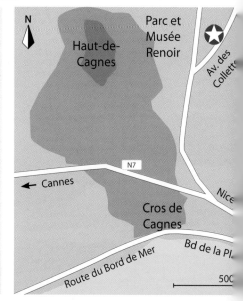

HIGHLIGHTS

- the medieval upper city with its impressive Grimaldi castle
- the Montée de la Bourgade

FACTS

Maps	IGN 3643 ET
Internet	www.cagnes-tourisme.com

Route — from the motorway A8 Nice-Cannes, take the exit Cagnes-sur-Mer. After that, take the road to Cagnes-Centre. Park

THE WALK

Via the Avenue Auguste Renoir and the Avenue Blériot, you take the Montée de la Bourgade **1** on the right. This very beautiful street that leads to the upper city, Haut-de-Cagnes. This street comes out exactly at the St-Pierreke a church from the early gothic style, which one enters via the pulpit, which is very rare indeed … It is best to exp the remainder of the upper city on your own. It is wonderful to parade through the little streets and on the s squares. You will arrive at the imposing castle of the Grimaldis anyway **3** …

The castle of the Grimaldis
The old upper city of Cagnes is dominated by the 14th century castle with its crenellations, built by Ranieri Grimalc king of Monaco. For centuries, this family ruled the region and every generation embellished and expanded the cast. During the French Revolution the family from Cagnes was driven out. Now the complexe houses a museum, who severe, medieval façade contrasts strongly with the lovely renaissance patio inside. On the ground floor, we find th Musée d'Olivier, amongst others, which provides an overview of the history of the olive cultivation and the olive (production processes.
On the first floor, we find the Suzy Solidor donation, about forty portraits of famous singers, made by the greate artists of the 20th century.
On the second floor, we have the museum for contemporary Mediterranean art, a collection of paintings of artists w lived at the Mediterranean coast.

HIGHLIGHTS

- superb panoramic views of the sea from green meadows

FACTS

Situation	halfway between Grasse and Vence
Maps	IGN 3643 ET
Internet	search word "Domaine de Courmettes"
Route	take the D2210 from Grasse or Vence. At a certain point, after Tourrettes-sur-Loup when come from Vence, before Tourrettes-sur-Loup if you come from Grasse komt, turn in at the ar marked "Domaine de Courmettes". You follow a tarred road that winds upwards. Drive rig the end and park in the centre (hotel and facilities for seminaries) "Domaine de Courmette

THE WALK

At the end of the parking lot (eastwards), you see a gravel road behind a barrier **1**. Follow it. You will now walk betw the green meadows, with the sea on the right, in the distance, and on the left the massif of the Pic de Courmettes continue eastwards, following the sloping road, which still runs more or less parallel with the coastline in the dista In front of you, you will see a mighty rock, the "Baou de Saint-Jeannet", with its steep southern face loom up ah You can then wander to the fields of Le Cairn **2**. Return along the same road.

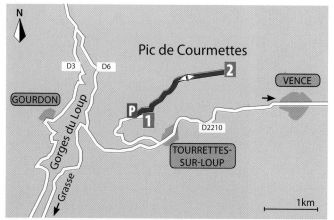

The Courmettes Domain
It is a remarkable landscape,
close to the Mediterranean Se
green meadows and oak fores
One would think you were in t
north of France, if it were not
the Mediterranean Sea that o
sees shimmering in the distar
… The Domaine de Courmettes
six-hundred-hectare sized natu
reserve in private ownership, b
open to the public. It is enclos
by the Gorges du Loup and t
valley of the river of the Loup.

2h. 100

- one of the most beautiful and deepes gorges in Frankrijk
- the Confiserie Florian

FACTS

Situation	the Gorges-du-Loup lie at about10km north of Grasse
Maps	IGN 3643 ET
Internet	search word « Gorges du Loup", www.confiserieflorian.com
Route	take the D2085 from Grasse and then the D2210 in the direction of Vence until you reach P. sur-Loup. Park in the village, on the parking lot next to the Loup river.

THE WALK

You will see the Confiserie Florian **1** at the side of the road. You walk upstream along a path along the river, betv the Confiserie and the river. You walk along the river in the deep valley for the whole journey, along little wate and over little bridges, until you reach the end of the path **2**. Return the same way.

The Gorges du Loup

The river rises at a height of 1300 metres high, in the limestone rocks near Grasse. Through its short loop, its flow is very intense and it has eroded an enormous gorge through the intensity with which it flows to the Mediterranean Sea. Its flow makes it quite spectacular.

The Confiserie Florian

receives visitors from all over the world, to get to know all the artisanal ways of producing jam, candied fruit and other sweets such as chocolate and Provençal sweets, which is a great speciality of South–France. There is also a boutique next to the workshop where you can, but are under no obligation to, buy.

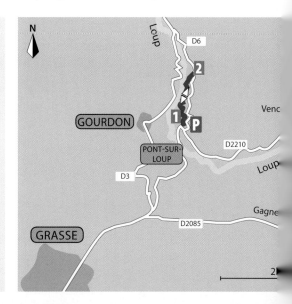

ANTIBES

- the archeological museum and the Picasso museum
- panoramic views of the lighthouse and of Garoupe
- the old city

FACTS

Situation	halfway between Cannes and Nice
Maps	IGN 3643 ET
Internet	www.antibesjuanlespins.com
Route	Park on one of the parking lots at the harbour of Port Vauban in Antibes.

THE WALK

At the Quai des Pêcheurs you walk into the old city via the gate "Porte Marine" **1**.
Go straight ahead (the Rue Aubernon, and, even further left, to the ramparts and the Promenade de l'Amiral de G
2. You follow this road that runs between the sea and the city walls. A bit further on, you turn right to the Place du
and the Museum of Picasso **3**, which has been housed in the old castle of the Grimaldis. You will also the Immac
Conception **4** Cathedral, which lies on a square a few metres lower down. You return to the Promenade and fol.
to the right, in the direction of Cap d'Antibes. You pass the archeological museum **5**, that is in the Bastion St-A
where many interesting items that were dug up in Antibes during the Roman period are exhibited (one of v
is a complete ship that transported sarcophagie). You continue walking over the embankent, along the Bd. Le
and the Plage de l'Ilette, the Plage de la Salis, until you get to the little harbour, Port de la Salis **6**. Here you turn
Chemin du Calvaire **7**, a "Calvary" path, with different stations, that starts on the other side of the little harbou
path rises to the Dame-de-la-Garoupe **8** church (two chapels that are connected to one another). There is al
orientation table, where you can enjoy a beautiful panoramic view from the Bay of Antibes to the Estérel Massif
Next to the church rises the lighthouse of Garoupe **9**. It is one of the most powerful lighthouses of the Mediterra
Sea and one may climb up it. On a clear day, you can see Corsica!
Return to the old city via the same route and, via the Rue de la Tourraque and the Cours Masséna, you walk unde
covered market back to the **10** Port Vauban.

Port
Vauban
P
1
2
10 3
4
VIEIL
ANTIBES

N

Baie des
Anges

Plage de L'Ilette

Plage de
la Salis
6

7

5

8 9
La Garoupe
500m

The Picasso museum

In 1946, Picasso spent the summer in Antibes. At that time, the Antibes museum was housed in the Grimaldi castle. The curator came up with a very original suggestion : he invited Picasso to use the castle as his studio during his stay in Antibes. Picasso found much inspiration and painted a great number of paintings, which all exude joie de vivre, the summer sun and wonder atmosphere.

Right next door, there is a more tragic story … Nicolas de Staél had isolated himself in a house in the city walls for six months, painted 350 beautiful paintings during this period, and then committed suicide. There is a great collection of both painters to be admired in this museum.

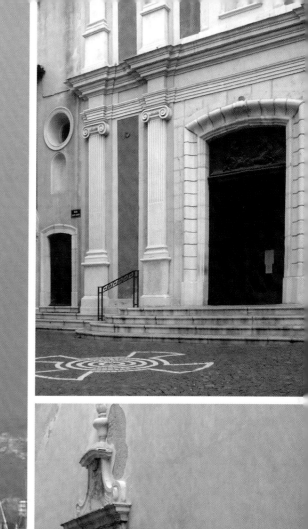

HIGHLIGHTS

- a magical, calming place that protrudes high from far out at sea

FACTS

Situation	5km south of Antibes
Maps	IGN 3643 ET
Internet	www.antibesjuanlespins.com
Route	take the D2559 to the coast from the centre of Antibes, to Plage de la Garoupe. Park on the parking lot behind the beach.

THE WALK

On the right, at the end of the beach, you will see the beginning of the coastal road. You pass Cap Gros **1** and walk up the around the rocks that have been eroded away and so around the peninsula. At a certain point the beach is barred by a You pass the passage in the wall and go up the path to the right. About 20 metres further on, you can go back on the l another passage and continue walking along the beach. You have lovely views of the Estérel Massif. At the Anse de l'A Faux **3**, the path is a dead end and you return until you get to the wall. You take the path in the direction of the interic turn left around the domain of Eilen Roc **4**. At the entrance of Eilen Roc, you turn right and reach the Bd. Fitzgerald Ker When you get here, you take the yellow-marked road and follow this until you reach the Plage de la Garoupe.

The coastal edges of Cap d'Antibes are littered with white, eroded dolomite rocks. Across this, there is a wonderful, rocky path, where you can only hear the rolling of the sea and the cry of the seagulls. The left there are gardens stretching from the domains out over the rocks. The peninsula's peace and quiet has inpired many an artist. Jules Verne wrote his "Two thousand leagues under the Sea" here. You pass the villa Eilen-Roc, which was built for the governor of Dutch India in 1867. It was built by the architect Garnier, who also built the Opera in Paris. There is a domain of eleven hectares around the villa that stretches to the sea. In the first half of the 20th century, Greta Garbo, King Farouk of Egypt, Léopold II of Belgium and Onassis were guests of the owner at the time, who was Hélène de Beaumont.

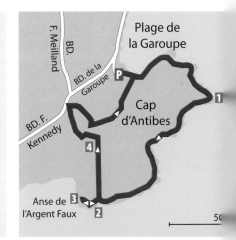

Sainte-Marguérite Island

the coastal path around the island, with divers panoramic views
the Royal fort – Le Musée de la Mer (can be visited)
the botanical track
the unspoilt beauty of nature

TS

ation	1km out to sea from the harbour Cannes.
s	IGN 3643 ET
rnet	search word "Ile Sainte-Marguérite"
te	Take the ferry (Tel (0033) (0) 493 39 11 82) in the old harbour of Cannes (Quai Maxime Laubeuf – Gare Maritime des Iles de Lérins). Sailing time is 15 minutes.

WALK

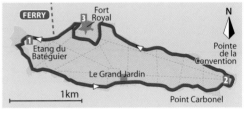

n you have arrived on the island from the walkway, the steps on the unpaved road on the right. At the Ju Batéguier **1**, leave the piste and walk around the lake in the direction of the bell. You automatically rn to the coastal road around the island.

inue following the coast, along the mighty 'sun rella' of pine trees to the furthest point of Ile Sainte-uerite **2**. Continue following the coastal road and enjoy the views of the bay and the Alps. Then you pass the Fort l **3** on the left (you can visit it). You automaticall return to the walkway.

nt or extra : from the walkway you can als follow the Sentier Botanique, where you will get an interesting overview e flora on the island. Signs with explanation and signposts are to be found everywhere.

Sainte-Marguerite

-Sainte-Marguerite forms « Les Iles de Lérins » together with Ile Saint-Honorat. According to the history writings, Les s de Lérins were a Roman city state. Recent diggings of mosaïcs, wall paintings and ceramics confirm this. Moreover, ere are Roman shipwrecks in front of the coast and the remains of a harbour have also been discovered. The little and is about 3km long and 1km wide. It is littered with pine and eucalyptus trees and the coasts are rocky. It is believable that one is only 1 km away from the cosmopolitan city of Cannes …

Fort Royal

vas built by Richelieu and Vauban at the end of 17th and the beginning of the 18th centuries. art from the fact that the mysterious Man with the Iron Mask was prisoner here, (possibly the illegitimate brother Louis XIV), the fort is interesting for its Musée de la Mer, with its archeological finds from the shipwrecks form the man era.

Ile Saint-Honorat.

HIGHLIGHTS

- one of the most important monasterial communities of Christian civilization
- beautiful panoramic views
- the wine, the liqueur …

INFO

Situation	1km out to sea from the harbour Cannes.
Maps	IGN 3643 ET
Internet	search word "Ile Saint-Honorat"
Route	Take the ferry (Tel (0033) (0) 493 39 11 82) in the old harbour of Cannes (Quai Maxime Laub – Gare Maritime des Iles de Lérins). Sailing time is 20 minutes.

Ile-Saint-Honorat

This island is only 1500 metres long and 400 metres wide, but has a great deal to offer. In the 4th century Sai Honoratius came to settle here. He founded on Lerina, the name for the island at the time, a monastery, which w to become one of the most important monasteries of Christian civilization. In the course of the centuries, it became popular place of pilgrimage and even popes came here barefoot on pilgrimage.

Seeing the monastery had to contend with many attacks from the Saracenes, a fortress was built on a little peninsu at the seaside. This functioned for a long time both as fortress for the soldiers, and as monastery. It later became jus monastery. It was built as we still know it today.

The whole island is the private ownership of this Cistercian community, but the monks have opened the island to t public. They produce wine and make liqueur. We also find seven chapels on the island, vineyards and olive gro and woods and see pines. There is also a shop where the monks sell their wine and liqueur, and where many religic books are sold.

THE WALK

When you arrive at the walkway **1**, you take the path to the right and walk anti-clockwise around the island. You first pass the chapel of Saint-Sauveur **2** on the left, then the Pointe du Barbier **3** with its chapel, and to the south of the monastery, **4** the fortress **5**. Finally, you turn around the island completely, round Pointe St-Féréol **6** and you reach the walkway once again.

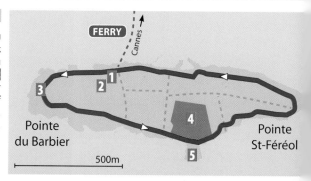

The Fontmerle pond and the Notre Dame-de-Vie chapel

HLIGHTS

the Notre-Dame-de-Vie chapel with avenue of cypruses
the fauna and flora of the Fontemerle lake

TS

ation	Mougins, 15km from Cannes
s	IGN 3643 ET
net	www.mougins-coteazur.org
e	from Mougins, you take the D35 in the direction of Antibes. You follow the signposting to the Hôtel "Le Manoir de l'Etang". You pass the entrance of the hotel and reach the Promenade de l'Etang. Park here.

WALK

sy meadows stretch out before your eyes, with, in the middle, the Fontemerle **1** lake. The little lake (5ha) is a true
ne" of flora (amongst others, the largest collection of lotus plants in Europe !) and fauna (more than 70 types of
!). You can watch nature from two observation points at the lake. You walk in an anti-clockwise direction around
ke. On your right, you will see the beautiful gardens of Le Manoir de l'Etang **2**.
ontinue on the road further south over the grassy fields, and get to a parking lot and there you turn right into
aussée de Picasso, that goes to the Notre-Dame-de-Vie chapel **3**. Here you think that you are in Tuscany. At this
ale place, an avenue of cypruses leads you to the 17th century chapel. It gets its name from the fact that, in the
the still-born children were baptized here. From 1961 to his death in 1973, Picasso lived in the hidden house
d "L'Antre du Minotaure".

ugins

e parson's nose ! A beautifully renovated little village
h Provençal and Italian atmosphere with refined
taurants and hotels. The residential area is one where
 can enjoy nature far from the busy coast.
ugins alone is worth a visit, but the immediate
roundings also have beautiful little secret places. You
k along the most beautiful holiday residences up
he idyllic little lake of Fontemerle, along the Notre-
ne-de-Vie chapel, bathing in a Toscan atmosphere,
h avenues of cypruses and Picasso's residence.

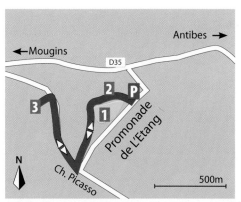